EARLY SKILLS LIBRARY

wonderful world

Developed by Macmillan Educational Company
Written by Lea and Victor Rangel-Ribeiro
Text illustrated by David Gantz
Educational Consultant—Marilyn LaPenta
Cover illustrated by Patrick Girouard

Newbridge Educational Programs

TABLE OF CONTENTS

SECTION ONE—ASIA

SECTION TWO—AFRICA AND AUSTRALIA

TABLE OF CONTENTS
Continued

BIRD IN THE CAGE
Japanese Song / Game

Bird in the cage, Bird in the cage, When will you come out and play? When will you come out to stay? Late in the eve-ning and clo-ser to dawn, I will stand be-hind you ear-ly in the morn.

You need: blindfold

Steps:

1. Explain to your class that children in Japan enjoy this song and game about a caged bird.

2. Teach children the song, one phrase at a time.

3. Then have children form a circle. Select one child to be "it" and stand blindfolded in the center of the circle.

4. The rest of the children skip around the circle as they sing the song, stopping where they are at the end of the song.

5. "It" then has three tries to guess the name of the child who stands directly behind him or her in the circle. If "it" guesses the correct name, that child becomes the new "it." If the child in the center does not guess the correct name after three tries, he or she selects another child to be "it."

6. The game continues as long as children's interest is sustained.

Variation:

In one version of this song, a turtle and a crane are also mentioned. Children can sing a second and third verse, substituting the words "Turtle in the pond" and "Crane in the nest" for "Bird in the cage."

ELF IN THE RIVER

According to Chinese folklore, after a rainy season elves live in rivers. They try to pull in people who are walking along the banks.

Steps:

1. Choose one child to be the elf.

2. Divide the rest of the class into two teams. The teams stand 10' apart in two parallel lines facing each other. (Older children can stand farther apart.) The two lines represent the river's banks.

3. The elf stands in the space between the teams. This area represents the river.

4. The elf calls out the name of a player on one of the river's banks.

5. That player then calls out the name of a player on the opposite bank of the river.

6. Both players try to cross the river to exchange places. They must reach their new places before being tagged by the elf.

7. The first player tagged by the elf becomes the new elf.

8. If no one is tagged, the game continues as described in steps 4 to 6, until a player is tagged.

9. Play the game for as long as it holds children's interest.

DRAGON CATCH-TAIL

The dragon is considered a symbol of good fortune in China. Chinese children hear dragon stories, use paper dragons in parades, and paint pictures of them.

Steps:

1. Have the players stand in a line, with one hand placed on the shoulder of the person in front and one hand placed on the shoulder of the person in back. The first in the line is the dragon's head, and the last is the tail.

2. To begin the game, have the "tail" shout, "One, two, three — come on, dragon!"

3. The dragon's "head" tries to catch the "tail," without causing any player to remove a hand from the next player's shoulder.

4. The dragon's "body" can twist and turn to keep the "head" from catching the "tail."

5. As soon as any player lets go of the next player's shoulder, that player breaks the dragon's body and a new dragon is formed. The "head" moves to the end of the line to become the "tail," and the next child in line becomes the "head."

6. Play continues for as long as the game holds children's interest.

THE GOATS, THE TIGER, AND THE JACKAL
Indian Folktale

Read the story below and on page 8 to the class. Then prepare the stick puppets as shown on pages 9 and 10. Retell the story, letting children use the puppets to dramatize it.

One fine summer evening, Father Goat, Mother Goat, and their three little kids were grazing high on a steep hillside, munching on fresh green grass. Suddenly a terrible rainstorm came up.

"What shall we do?" asked Father Goat. "It's getting late, the sky is dark, and the streams will be flooded. We'll have trouble getting home by nightfall."

"Look! There's a nice warm spot," said Mother Goat, pointing to a nearby cave. "Let's go inside and wait out the storm. In the morning, when the sun comes out, we'll continue on our way."

"But it's a tiger's cave," said Father Goat.

"Oh, he's out hunting now," said his wife. "We must just make sure we leave before he comes back."

"What if we meet him on the way?" asked Father Goat.

"He'll be so full from his dinner, he won't bother us" she said. And so the goat family trotted off into the warm and comfortable cave. Soon the little kids and their father were fast asleep. Only Mother Goat was awake as the great big tiger came huffing and puffing up the hill. The tiger had had a bad night hunting and had caught nothing for his meal. Tired and hungry, he decided to go home earlier than usual. "Huff, pant, puff," went the tiger, stopping every few yards to rest.

"Wake up, Father Goat, wake up quickly!" Mother Goat whispered. "I hear the tiger climbing up the hill. What shall we do now?"

"I have a plan," said Father Goat, thinking out loud. "This cave has a great echo. We can make our voices sound very loud. Together we can scare the tiger so badly he will run away and leave us alone." And he continued to tell Mother Goat his plan.

Mother Goat waited till the tiger was 15 yards from the mouth of the cave before she pinched the kids awake. They bleated loudly.

The tiger stopped at once. "Aha!" he thought, "a little goat family. What a delicious breakfast they will make! I wonder where they are." And he crept forward a few feet and waited.

Meanwhile, Mother Goat pinched the kids once more, and they bleated louder than before.

"What luck!" thought the hungry tiger, licking his whiskers. "What absolutely wonderful luck! They're right here, in my own cave. I wonder who else is in there?" And he crept even closer. What the tiger heard next was a voice so loud and terrifying it made his hair stand on end.

"Why are the children crying?" the loud voice boomed. It was Father Goat's voice. Tiger didn't know that. He thought he heard a monster.

"The children want to eat fresh tiger meat for breakfast," roared Mother Goat's equally loud voice.

"Give them what's left of yesterday's tiger," shouted Father Goat.

"They don't want it. They want fresh tiger meat today," yelled Mother Goat.

"Then bring me my big sharp hunting knife," roared Father Goat. "There's a nice, plump tiger outside our cave right now, with enough meat on him to last us till tomorrow."

The tiger was now so frightened that he didn't wait to hear any more. He rushed down the hill, tumbling and rolling as he tried to reach safety. Halfway down the hill he was stopped by a cunning jackal, who had his den hidden behind some bushes.

"Where are you going in such a hurry, Tiger?" asked the jackal politely. "Has something scared you?"

"You'd be scared too if you met the monsters who are now living in my cave," answered the tiger.

The jackal suspected that the tiger had only heard a loud echo. He said, "If I help you get those monsters, and you have them for breakfast, can I have what's left over for lunch?"

"Of course," said the tiger. "But how do I know you won't leave me when the monster comes out with the knife?"

"How do I know you won't leave me?" answered the jackal. So they decided to tie their tails together so neither could leave the other. Then they marched up the hill to the cave. As they got closer they heard a loud noise.

"Why are the children crying?" boomed Father Goat.

"They want fresh tiger meat for breakfast," roared Mother Goat.

"Tell them they're in luck, and pass me my hunting knife. They can have not only fresh tiger meat but jackal stew as well."

And with that, Father Goat drummed his hooves on the floor of the cave. The echo made it sound as loud as a thunderclap. The jackal became as frightened as the tiger. Together, with their tails still tied, they turned and scrambled down the hill, bumping into rocks and thorns. They never stopped till they were many miles away. The tiger never returned to his cave. The jackal never returned to his den. To this day tigers don't come too close to villages where goats live. Jackals, though they come closer, never come close enough to be turned into jackal stew!

THE GOATS, THE TIGER, AND THE JACKAL
Stick Puppets / Cutouts

You need: puppet cutouts on this page and page 10
crayons or markers
glue
oaktag
scissors
ice-cream sticks

Steps:

1. Reproduce the puppet cutouts on this page and page 10, making one copy each of the tiger and jackal, and five copies of the goat.

2. Distribute the cutouts to seven children, and have them color the tiger orange, the jackal gray, and the goats brown.

3. Then have children glue the cutouts onto oaktag and cut them out. Assist them in cutting around the goats' horns if necessary.

4. To make handles for the puppets, glue an ice-cream stick onto the back of each one, so that about half the stick extends beyond the bottom of the puppet.

5. Retell the story of "The Goats, the Tiger, and the Jackal," letting children use the puppets to act out the story.

THE GOATS, THE TIGER, AND THE JACKAL
Cutouts

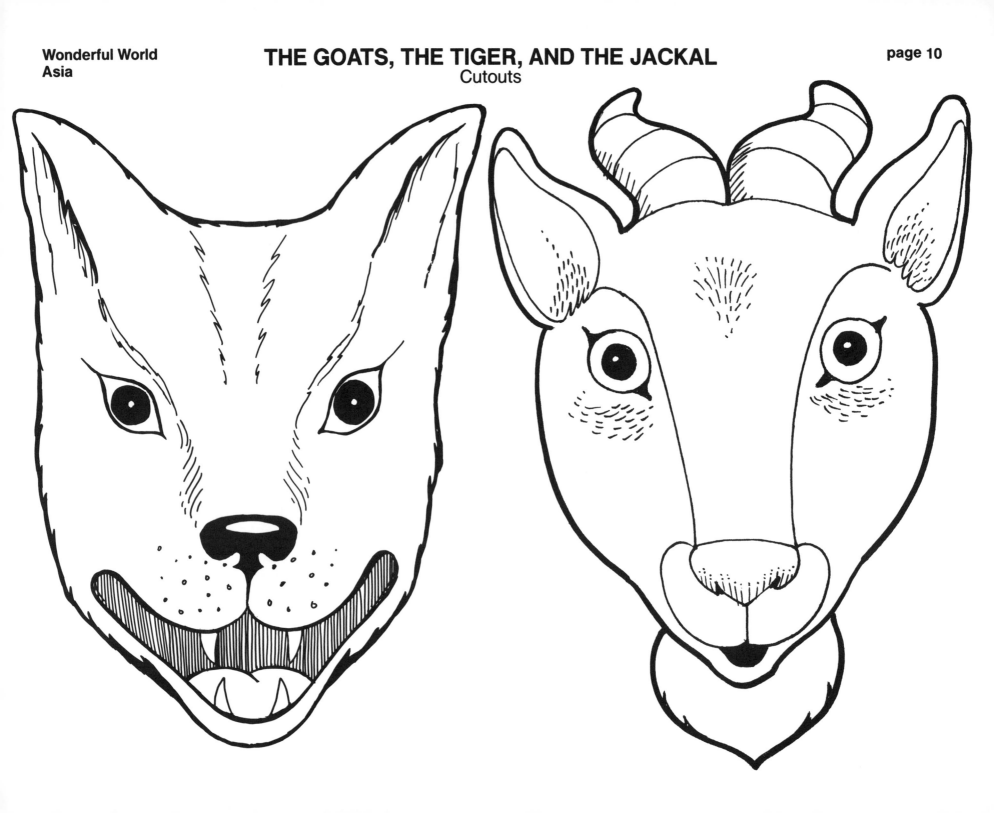

LADDOOS

Ingredients: ¼ cup dark brown sugar
1 cup water
4 cups puffed rice
¼ teaspoon ground cardamom
1 teaspoon crystallized ginger

How to Make:

1. Pour sugar into a medium-sized pan and place over very low heat, stirring constantly, until it liquefies.

2. Gradually add water and stir to form a syrup.

3. Test for doneness by allowing a drop or two of the syrup to fall into cold water. The syrup is ready for use when the cooled syrup forms a soft ball as it is rolled between the thumb and forefinger.

4. Remove the syrup from the heat.

5. Spread one cup puffed rice, completely flattened, on a cookie sheet. Spread a pinch of the cardamom, ¼ teaspoon ginger, and several tablespoons of the syrup over the puffed rice.

6. Roll the mixture into an elongated sausage shape. Cut it into four or five sections, each the size of a walnut. Carefully form each into a ball.

7. Place the laddoos on a cookie sheet, allowing them to cool and harden for 15 minutes before eating or storing.

8. Repeat steps 5 through 7 three more times. (Makes 20 laddoos.)

KULFI (Indian ice cream)

Ingredients: 1 quart milk
½ pint heavy cream
¼ cup sugar
½ cup chopped pistachio nuts
½ cup chopped almonds
1 tablespoon vanilla
2 drops red food coloring

How to Make:

1. Combine milk and heavy cream in a saucepan.

2. Simmer over medium heat for about 20 minutes until thick.

3. Add sugar, pistachio nuts, almonds, vanilla, and food coloring. Mix thoroughly. Let cool.

4. Fill small paper cups halfway with kulfi and place in a freezer for one hour until the kulfi has the consistency of soft sherbet. (Makes ten servings.)

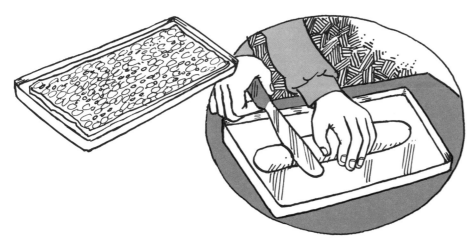

TIGER IN THE DEN

You need: chalk

Steps:

1. Clear a play area on the playground approximately 20′ × 20′.

2. Use a piece of chalk to mark an **X** on each of the four corners of the play area. Each **X** is a base.

3. Choose one child to be the "tiger." The tiger stands on any base while the rest of the children form a tight circle in the center of the square. They hold hands and chant the following lines while moving in a circle:

   The tiger's not here,
   The tiger's not here,
   The tiger is prowling around.
   We run and hide
   When the tiger roars,
   For he makes such a frightening sound.

4. During the chanting and circling, the tiger moves from one base to another. After the children complete the verse, the tiger must stay put until he or she roars. The tiger's roar is the signal for the other players to run to any base as the tiger chases them. Players must try to reach a base before being tagged by the tiger.

5. The first player tagged by the tiger before reaching a base becomes the tiger in the next round. Continue the game for as long as it holds children's interest.

CHEETAH, CHEETAL

You need: chalk

Steps:

1. Explain to children that the *cheetah* is a large, spotted member of the cat family that once lived in India. The cheetah runs very fast and hunts deer, among other prey. The *cheetal* is a quick-footed, spotted deer found in India. Then let children play this running game.

2. With chalk, draw two parallel lines about 6′ apart and 12′ long in the middle of the play area. These are the starting lines. Then draw parallel lines at either end of the play area, making these lines about 20′ from the center lines. These are the home bases.

3. Divide the class into two equal teams—the cheetahs and the cheetals. If there is an even number of children in your class, you can be the caller for the game. If you have an odd number of children in your class, let one child be the caller.

4. Ask the teams to stand along the center lines, backs to each other. The caller stands between the two teams, but to one side.

5. The caller shouts "Cheeeeee—" and then ends suddenly with "–tah" or "–tal." The members of each team must listen carefully to hear which team's name is called.

6. The players on the team whose name is called race toward their home base while the children on the other team turn around and chase their opponents, trying to tag them before reaching the home base. A player who is tagged before reaching his or her home base must drop out of the game.

7. The remaining players then line up again along the starting lines, and the game is repeated. Play continues until all the members of one team are out and the other team becomes the winner.

MIDDLE EASTERN TREATS
Recipes

For tasty Middle Eastern snacks, let children help prepare these holiday treats.

HAMANTASCHEN FROM ISRAEL

Children in Israel eat hamantaschen on the holiday of Purim. A hamantaschen is a pastry that represents the hat worn by the evil Haman, who plotted against the ancient Jews. Today, Israeli children dress in costumes, parade in the streets, and have parties on Purim.

Ingredients: 7 tablespoons butter or margarine
⅓ cup sugar
two eggs
2½ cups flour
¼ cup orange juice
1 teaspoon lemon juice
one jar prune or plum jam

How to Make:

1. Cream the butter or margarine and sugar together in a large bowl.

2. Separate the eggs. Discard the whites. Add the yolks and mix.

3. Add the flour and juices and mix to form dough.

4. On a floured board, roll out the dough to about ⅛″ thickness.

5. Use a cookie cutter to cut into 4″ circles.

6. Spoon a tablespoon of jam into the center of each circle and fold up three edges to create a triangle shape. Leave a small opening at the center. (Other fillings, such as poppy seeds or apricot jam, can be used.)

7. Press the edges together to form a three-cornered pastry. (See illustration.)

8. Place on cookie sheet and bake for 20 minutes at 350°F. (Makes 16 to 20 hamantaschen.)

TURKISH HOLIDAY PILAF

Ingredients: 4 oz. butter or margarine
2 cups long-grain rice
4 cups chicken broth
1 teaspoon salt
2 tablespoons blanched almonds
2 tablespoons pitted dates
2 tablespoons raisins

How to Make:

1. Melt butter or margarine in a large frying pan.

2. Add uncooked rice and stir over medium heat for 2 minutes or until all the grains are coated.

3. Add chicken broth and salt.

4. Bring to a boil. Then lower heat, cover, and cook for about 15 minutes, or until all liquid is absorbed.

5. Toss the rice pilaf mixture with a fork.

6. Chop almonds and dates coarsely with a knife and stir into the pilaf.

7. Sprinkle raisins on top.

8. Serve in small paper cups with spoons or forks. (Makes 12 servings.)

BAFTA HINDI
Saudi Arabian Song / Game

Baf - ta Hin - di, In - di - an fab - rics: Sa - tins, silks, and jew - els too!

Ma - ny things for each and ev - 'ry one, Come and buy them just for you!

Ma - ny things for each and ev - 'ry one, Come and buy them just for you!

You need: basket filled with trinkets, pieces of fabric, buttons, costume jewelry

Steps:

1. Explain to children that "Bafta Hindi" is sung in Saudi Arabia by merchants in the markets as they sell their wares.

2. Teach the two verses of the song to the class, one line at a time. When children are familiar with the words and music, have them stand in a circle, facing the center.

3. Select one child to be the Saudi Arabian merchant. Have that child stand inside the circle with the basket filled with objects to sell. As the class sings the song, the merchant walks around the circle, holding up various objects in the basket to show the class.

4. At the end of the first verse, the merchant selects another child to hold the basket. This child walks around the circle as the second verse is sung.

Follow-up Activity:

Help children create their own verses to "Bafta Hindi," in which they include additional objects to sell. Gather these objects and place them in the basket. Then sing the new verses and play the game again.

<u>Verse 2</u>

Come and look into my basket,
You'll find many shiny things.
There are buttons, rings, and bracelets,
Come and buy them just for you!
Many things for each and ev'ry one,
Come and buy them just for you!

Read the story below to your class. Then reproduce the worksheet on page 16 for children to complete.

Long, long ago, in a village in Burma that sat near the edge of the forest, there lived four boys who were friends. When they grew up, three of them left the village to study at a college in the big city. The fourth one stayed behind to work in the fields as a farmer. When the three young men, who were now scholars, returned to their village, they felt they had learned a great deal and were very wise. They thought that their fourth friend, the farmer, was a fool because he had not studied in the big city.

One day all four friends went into the forest to hunt for tigers. Although they moved quietly and went to all the places where a tiger would probably be, they found no tigers, none at all.

Just as they were about to leave the forest, one of the scholars saw a heap of tiger bones lying under some leaves.

"Let me put them together to form a tiger skeleton," he said. "It's one of the many skills I learned in college. And I do it very well." And indeed he did. He put together a splendid skeleton of a tiger.

The second scholar found a dried tiger skin. "Just what I need!" he cried. "If I wrap this skin around the bones, everyone will think this is a real tiger. This is one of the things I learned to do in college. And I do it very well." He did it so well that all four of them gathered around in awe, thinking what a splendid, fierce tiger it would have been. If only the tiger were truly alive!

The third scholar then took a step forward. "I can do it," he said. "I can bring this tiger to life."

"Don't, please don't!" pleaded the farmer. "If you do, it will eat us all up!"

"Nonsense! You are a very foolish farmer," answered the third scholar. "If I bring it to life, I will be its master. It dare not eat me up, nor will it dare harm my friends."

But the farmer had already climbed the tallest tree he could find. From there, he watched the third scholar bring the tiger to life.

"At last, you're real, you're a very real tiger!" said the scholar. "Thank me, Tiger!"

"I'm not only a real tiger but a very hungry tiger," said the beast. "And I thank you not only for giving me life but for providing me with a meal as well."

And one, two, three, before they could even blink their eyes twice, the tiger ate up all three of the scholars. Now, who was wise, and who was foolish?

Discussion Questions:

1. Where did the four friends live?

2. What did three of the four friends become when they grew up?

3. What did the fourth friend become when he grew up?

4. What did the first scholar learn to do at college? the second scholar? the third?

5. Why were the three scholars the real fools in this story?

THE FARMER IN THE TREE
Worksheet

Name_____

Look at the Color Key at the bottom of the page.
Match the colors in the key with the numbers in the picture.
Then color the picture.

Color Key: 1=brown   2=green   3=yellow   4=blue   5=orange

Tell children that blue and white are the colors of the Israeli flag. A star with six points, the Star of David, is also on the flag. Explain to your class that the Hebrew word *shalom* has several meanings: "hello"; "good-bye"; "peace be with you." Have children make the greeting card described on this page. They may send their cards to friends or relatives in honor of Rosh Hashanah, the Jewish New Year (celebrated in September).

You need: oaktag
ruler
pencils
scissors
light blue construction paper
6″ × 9″ pieces of white construction paper
glue
crayons or fine-line markers

Steps:

1. On oaktag, measure and draw an equilateral triangle with 3″ sides. Cut it out and trace it several more times onto oaktag. Then cut out the triangles.

2. Have each child trace an oaktag triangle pattern two times onto light blue construction paper and then cut out the paper triangles.

3. Give each child a 6″ × 9″ piece of white construction paper. Ask children to fold their papers in half to make 6″ × 4½″ cards.

4. To make the six-pointed Star of David, each child first glues one paper triangle, point up, onto the center of the front of his or her card. He or she then lays the second triangle on top of the first triangle, positioning it so that the point of the second triangle overlaps the bottom of the first triangle. (See illustration.) Have the child glue the second triangle in place.

5. Write the word *Shalom* on the chalkboard. Ask children to copy the word onto the top fronts of their cards, using crayons or fine-line markers. Assist children if necessary.

6. Children may then decorate their cards by drawing trees and flowers around the Star of David. Inside their cards, children can write brief messages and sign their names.

CELEBRATING THE NEW YEAR IN IRAN
Writing Activity / Science Activity

THE SEVEN S'S

You need: seven common objects whose names begin
with the letter S, such as stapler, sock,
skate, spoon, scarf, stamp, or seeds
writing paper
pencils
chalk
worksheet on page 19

Steps:

1. Explain that children in Iran celebrate the New Year for 13 days starting on March 21. A festival table is prepared with seven good luck objects. The names of these objects all start with the letter S.

2. Bring in seven objects or ask children to bring in objects whose names begin with the letter S. When seven different objects are collected, distribute paper and pencils. Have individual children take turns holding up one object, and have the rest of the class say its name.

3. Older children will copy the names of the objects as you write them on the chalkboard to create a lucky "Seven S's" list. Then they can illustrate their lists.

4. Younger children can write the letter S at the tops of their papers and draw pictures of the seven objects shown.

5. Display the lucky "Seven S's" lists on a bulletin board.

6. Reproduce the worksheet on page 19 for each child to complete.

Variation:

Provide seven objects whose names begin with another lucky letter and two objects whose names do not begin with that letter. Hold up the objects one at a time, in random order. Have children name the objects and determine which of the seven are the lucky objects.

THIRTEENTH DAY OUT

You need: cheesecloth
scissors
small plastic-foam meat trays (one for each child)
water
dried lima, kidney, or lentil beans
dark marker
storage-sized plastic bags with ties (one for each child)
worksheet on page 20

Steps:

1. Explain that on the thirteenth day of the New Year celebration in Iran, everyone goes to the countryside for a picnic. People bring green sprouts with them that they have grown at home, for good luck and long life. On this day, they throw the sprouts into a stream, to symbolize the start of the new year in peace and friendship.

2. For each child, cut pieces of cheesecloth to cover the bottom of the trays in triple thickness.

3. Add enough water to each tray to moisten the cheesecloth.

4. Have each child place four beans close together on the cheesecloth. Each child then writes his or her name on the side of the tray and slips it inside a plastic bag. Help children tie the plastic bags securely to make them as airtight as possible.

5. Children will place their trays in a sunny area near a window and check them every day. If any cheesecloth dries, open the plastic bag and add a small amount of water. Then retie it. (It is best not to add water unless absolutely necessary, as beans may become soggy and rot.) Beans will start to sprout in about one week.

6. Have children record their beans' progress. Reproduce the "Bean Growth Chart" on page 20 for each child. Distribute the charts on the days named. Children will draw pictures depicting their plants' growth.

Name_____

After you learn about New Year's in Iran, look at the picture
of the toy store below. Find seven objects that start with the letter S.
Circle each object. Then color in the picture.

BEAN GROWTH CHART
Worksheet

Name _____

Look at the chart below.
Draw a picture of your beans to show how they look
on each of the days named.

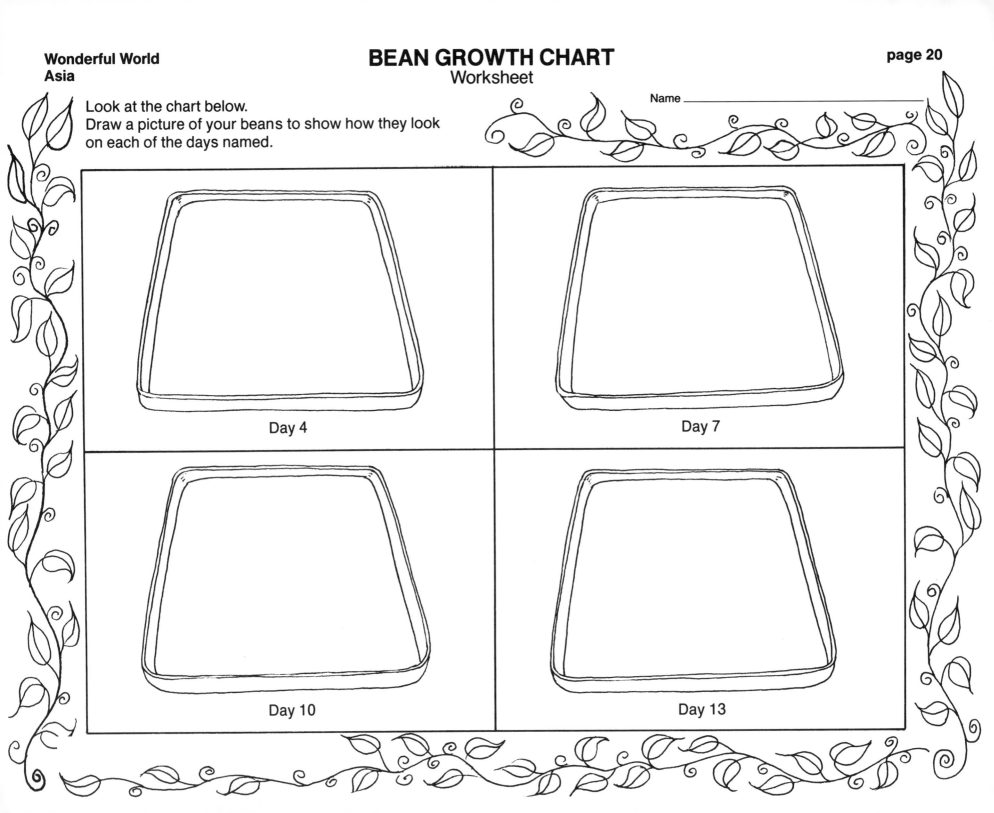

Day 4

Day 7

Day 10

Day 13

A FAIR IN PAKISTAN
Worksheet

Name_____

Children in Pakistan go to the fair at the end of the month-long holiday of Ramadan. They enjoy picnics with their families and have fun at the fair.

Look at the picture of the fairground below.
Color the two camels yellow.
Color the dancing bear brown.
Color the parrot red.
Circle the three acrobats.
Draw a line under the monkey.

DRAGON LANTERNS
Vietnamese Art Activity / Pattern

You need: pattern on this page
scissors
pencils
12″ × 18″ brightly colored
   construction paper
ruler
stapler
dark marker

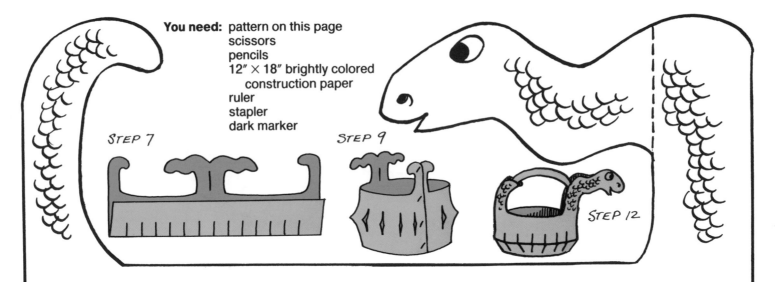

STEP 7

STEP 9

STEP 12

This Side at Fold

Steps:

1. Explain that the happiest holiday of the year for Vietnamese children is Tet Trung-Thu, the Mid-Autumn Festival. At that time children make lanterns in rabbit, fish, dragon, bird, or boat shapes. They parade with them in the streets to the sounds of music.

2. Reproduce the pattern on this page for each child and for yourself.

3. Have each child cut out the pattern along the solid line and trace it onto construction paper that is folded into a 12″ × 9″ rectangle. Make sure children place the edge of the pattern marked "This Side at Fold" at the folded edge of the construction paper.

4. Each child will then cut out a construction paper lantern.

5. Have each child unfold the paper to reveal a mirror-image dragon body shape that is 4″ × 16″.

6. Demonstrate how to fold the bottom part of the lantern up, in half.

7. Starting at the fold of the paper, show children how to measure and draw lines that are 1″ long and 1″ apart. Then have children fold their papers and draw lines. See illustration.

8. Ask children to cut along the lines, beginning at the folded edges.

9. Next, each child will unfold the paper and bend it into a cylinder. Staple the side edges of each child's lantern together, as shown.

10. To make handles for the lanterns, cut 1″ × 10″ strips of construction paper; staple a strip in an arc to the top of each lantern.

11. Have children fold the two dragon heads facing away from the body of the lantern along the neck where the dotted lines appear on the pattern. Staple the heads together.

12. With dark markers, children can draw the dragons' faces and scales .

dragon pattern

Make the flannel board characters described on pages 25 and 26 and use them to dramatize this story as
you read it to your class. You may wish to identify each animal character before beginning the story.

Early one morning, Lizard was drinking water at a water hole. Mosquito flew up to whisper something in his ear.

"You won't believe what I saw yesterday, Lizard," Mosquito said.

"What did you see?" asked Lizard.

"I saw a farmer digging yams out of the ground. Big yams." Mosquito knew that Lizard loved yams.

"Oh?" he said. "Big yams? How big?"

"As big as me. Hee-hee-hee," laughed Mosquito.

But Lizard did not think this was funny. In fact, he became angry. "Who wants to listen to such nonsense?" he asked, stuffing two fingers in his ears. Then off he went, mumbling angrily to himself.

"Mosquito was trying to make a fool of me," Lizard said. Python lay curled in the grass as Lizard passed by.

"Good morning," called Python, happily. But Lizard did not answer. He walked on, still grumbling.

"Oh, oh," thought Python. "I don't know why, but Lizard is angry with me. And he is dangerous when he's angry. Where can I hide?"

Finding a rabbit hole, Python went right in without knocking. When Rabbit saw Python enter her house, she ran out the back door, as fast as she could. Crow, who saw Rabbit running, flapped her wings and flew quickly into the forest.

"Caw! Caw! Caw! Danger! Danger!" cried Crow. Monkey heard Crow and helped to spread the alarm.

"Eek! Eek!" cried Monkey, as he jumped from tree to tree. "Danger! Run and hide!"

When Monkey jumped on a dry branch where Mother Owl had made her nest, it broke and fell. Mother Owl's nest, with Baby Owlet inside, went tumbling to the ground. Baby Owlet was so frightened he ran away. When Mother Owl came home and found her nest on the ground and Baby Owlet gone, she became very sad.

"Where is my baby?" she asked. "Who broke the branch my nest rested on?"

"Monkey did it," the other animals in the forest said. "He jumped on this branch, and it broke and fell." Mother Owl became sadder still.

Now it was the rule in the forest that Mother Owl had to hoot each morning, to wake up the sun. The sun could then rise, and day would begin.

The next morning, Mother Owl was too sad to hoot. So the sun did not wake up and rise, and night became longer and longer. The animals became afraid that the sun would become angry, go away, and never come back.

So King Lion called a meeting. All the animals came and sat in a circle. Mother Owl sat very sadly.

"Why haven't you hooted so the sun will wake up and day can begin?" asked King Lion.

"Because Monkey made my nest fall and Baby Owlet ran away and is lost. This made me sad," said Mother Owl. "When I'm sad, I cannot hoot."

"Monkey," roared King Lion, "why did you do that?"

"I was trying to help all the animals, O King!" said Monkey. "I heard Crow crying 'Danger!' so I jumped from tree to tree crying 'Danger!' too. That's when a branch broke and Mother Owl's nest fell."

"Crow," cried King Lion, "why did you frighten Monkey?"

"I saw Rabbit running," said Crow. "She was very frightened. That frightened me, too."

"Rabbit, why did you frighten Crow?"

"Python came hissing into my house, Mighty King!" said Rabbit. "Python moved so fast, I had to run."

"Python, why did you frighten Rabbit?"

"I said 'Good morning' to Lizard," said Python, "but he just walked on, muttering to himself. That scared me."

"Why didn't you answer Python, Lizard?" asked King Lion. But Lizard could not hear the question because he still had his fingers in his ears. Two friends pulled Lizard's fingers out of his ears, and King Lion repeated his question.

"I did not hear Python, O Great King," said Lizard, bowing low. "Mosquito had whispered nonsense into my ears, and that upset me. I stuck my fingers into my ears, so I could not hear him at all."

"Mosquito is such a pest," cried all the animals. "He bothers us, too!" Mosquito was afraid of King Lion's anger. He flew off and hid in the grass.

Just then, Baby Owlet poked his head out from under a bush. Mother Owl smiled and was happy again. She hooted and the sun came up. Now when Mosquito sees human beings, he flies close to our ears.

"Are you angry with me also?" he buzzes. We slap our cheeks to show that we are.

WHY MOSQUITOES BUZZ
Flannel Board Characters

You need: animal cutouts on this page and page 26
glue
oaktag
scissors
fine-line markers
felt scraps
flannel board

Steps:

1. Reproduce the animal cutouts on this page and page 26.

2. Glue them onto oaktag and cut them out.

3. Color the animals with fine-line markers.

4. Glue a small piece of felt onto the back of each cutout.

5. Use the animal cutouts on the flannel board to dramatize the story "Why Mosquitoes Buzz" on pages 23 and 24.

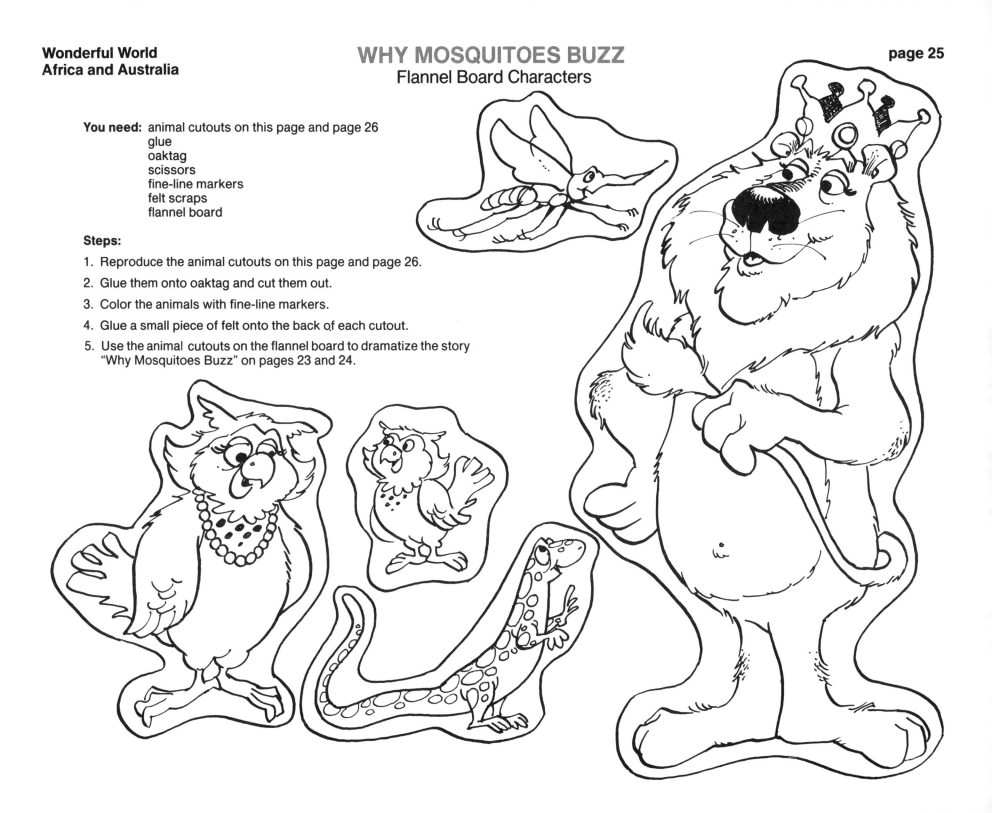

EVERYBODY LOVES SATURDAY NIGHT
Nigerian Song

Steps:

1. Explain to children that this popular Nigerian folk song has been translated into many languages and has been sung by people all over the world.

2. Have the children sit in a circle. Teach them the words to the song. Then have them clap out the beat as they sing.

3. Next teach children any or all of the translated versions listed below. Ask individual children to pick a version they would like the class to sing.

English

Everybody loves Saturday night.
Everybody loves Saturday night.
Everybody, everybody, everybody, everybody,
Everybody loves Saturday night.

French

Tout le monde aime samedi soir.
Tout le monde aime samedi soir.
Tout le monde, tout le monde, tout le monde, tout le monde,
Tout le monde aime samedi soir.

Spanish

A todos les gusta la noche del sábado.
A todos les gusta la noche del sábado.
A todos les gusta, a todos les gusta, a todos les gusta,
*   a todos les gusta,*
A todos les gusta la noche del sábado.

Chinese

Ren ren si huan li pai lu.
Ren ren si huan li pai lu.
Ren ren si huan, ren ren si huan, ren ren si huan, ren ren si huan,
Ren ren si huan li pai lu.

Russian

Vsiem nravitsa sabbota vietcheram.
Vsiem nravitsa sabbota vietcheram.
Vsiem nravitsa, vsiem nravitsa, vsiem nravitsa, vsiem nravitsa,
Vsiem nravitsa sabbota vietcheram.

PEANUT SOUP (Nigeria)

Ingredients: one large potato
one medium-sized onion
one large tomato
2 cups water
one beef bouillon cube
1 teaspoon salt
½ cup peanut butter
½ cup milk
2 tablespoons uncooked rice

How to Make:

1. Peel the potato and the onion. Then chop them and the tomato into small pieces.

2. Place vegetables in a large saucepan. Add water, bouillon cube, and salt.

3. Cover the saucepan and bring the mixture to a boil. Then reduce heat and simmer for 20 minutes.

4. In a small bowl mix the peanut butter and the milk until smooth. Add to the mixture in the saucepan and stir.

5. Stir in the rice, and continue to simmer for 30 minutes, or until rice is cooked. (Makes about ten half-cup servings.)

COUSCOUS (North Africa)

Ingredients: 1⅓ cups couscous (wheat grain semolina)
¾ cup raisins
¼ teaspoon salt
1 cup water
½ cup butter
¼ teaspoon ground turmeric

How to Make:

1. Combine the couscous, raisins, and salt in a medium-sized bowl.

2. Boil the water in a saucepan, then remove from heat. Stir in the couscous mixture and let stand until all the water is absorbed.

3. Melt butter in a large saucepan. Stir in the couscous mixture.

4. Add turmeric to the mixture and cook 3 to 4 minutes over low heat, uncovered. Couscous can be served with chicken or vegetables arranged around it. (Makes about ten half-cup servings.)

Read the story of "The Rabbits and the Crocodile" to your class and discuss the questions on page 30.
Then have children complete the worksheet on page 31.

Papa Rabbit, Mama Rabbit, and five baby rabbits lived not far from the banks of the Congo River. And on the banks of the river itself lived a big, green, very mean crocodile.

One day, quite early in the morning, Papa Rabbit went looking for food for his hungry family. He thought they might enjoy a breakfast of fine plantain leaves. On the way he passed their neighbor, Mr. Goat.

"Good morning, Mr. Goat," said Papa Rabbit.

"Good morning," said Mr. Goat. "Where are you going, so bright and early?"

"To the riverbank," said Papa Rabbit, "to bring home a fine breakfast of plantain leaves for my family."

"Be careful," said Mr. Goat. "I saw the big, green, very mean crocodile sleeping there with his snout in the middle of the leaves."

"I will," said Papa Rabbit, and he continued on his way.

When he reached the riverbank, he saw the big, green, very mean crocodile. As Mr. Goat had said, the crocodile was asleep with his snout in the middle of the plantain leaves.

"Kind Crocodile," said Papa Rabbit, very politely, "won't you please move aside a little? I want to gather a few of these plantain leaves for my children's breakfast."

"Those are my leaves," said Crocodile nastily. "I'm using them for a pillow. Now go away, before I have you for breakfast."

Papa Rabbit hopped back a few steps to think. It had been a cold, foggy morning, but now that the sun was up, he could see the mist rising like smoke from the middle of the river. And that gave him an idea.

Quickly, Papa Rabbit hopped home and explained his plan to his family. Together they gathered some dry leaves, which Papa Rabbit rolled up into a little bundle.

Then they all headed for the riverbank. They stopped a short distance from where the big, green, very mean crocodile was sleeping.

"Stay here," said Papa Rabbit to his family, "until I give you the sign. Then you know what to do."

Papa Rabbit hopped forward till he stood right in front of Crocodile. He placed his little roll of leaves on the ground and set fire to it. The smoke blew right into the sleeping crocodile's face. Soon, Crocodile's snout began to twitch. When he saw that, Papa Rabbit gave his family the secret sign. Mama and the five baby rabbits now tiptoed forward, and when they were close enough they began to run quickly around Crocodile shouting, "Fire! Fire!" as loudly as they could.

Crocodile opened one eye, smelled the smoke, and saw what he thought were hundreds of rabbits running in a panic all around him.

"This could become a bad forest fire," he thought. "I'd better get into the water quickly and stay there. In the river, no fire can touch me." And in one mad rush he scrambled straight to the water and slid in, as the rabbits scurried to get out of his way.

And that is why crocodiles spend so much time in the river and why rabbits eat all the plantain leaves they can find. Rabbits and other animals still keep their eyes wide open when they go down to the river for a drink of water, since a crocodile just might be there, waiting for them.

Discussion Questions:

1. Why was Papa Rabbit going to the riverbank?

2. Whom did Papa Rabbit meet on the way to the riverbank?

3. What was Papa Rabbit's idea for getting Crocodile to move?

4. What gave Papa Rabbit that idea?

5. Why do crocodiles spend so much time in the river?

THE RABBITS AND THE CROCODILE
Worksheet

Connect the dots from 1 to 15 to see where the crocodile is hiding.
Then color the picture.

Name_____

Name_____

Each animal shown below is missing something.
Read and follow the directions in each box.
Then cut the pictures apart and staple them together to make a minibook.

Draw black stripes on the zebra.

Draw a trunk on the elephant.
Color the elephant gray.

Color the giraffe yellow.
Draw brown spots on the giraffe.

Draw a hump on the camel.
Color the camel light brown.

BEANS IN A BOWL (West Africa)

You need: chalk
yardstick
large metal or plastic bowl
30 dried beans
three paper cups

Steps:

1. Chalk a 2' line on the floor or playground surface.

2. Place the bowl 4' from the tossing line.

3. Divide the class into groups of three. If there are children left over, those children can be scorekeepers.

4. Three children play at a time. Give each of two players 15 beans in a paper cup. Give the third player only a paper cup.

5. The first player will stand behind the chalked line and toss the beans underhand, one by one, trying to get each of them into the bowl. He or she will then collect any beans tossed into the bowl and place them back in the cup. Any beans that fall outside the bowl remain on the floor.

6. The second player will then take a turn trying to get his or her beans into the bowl in the same manner as the first player.

7. The third player then picks up any beans scattered on the floor and, standing behind the chalked line, tries to toss them into the bowl one at a time. If the third player succeeds in getting all the beans into the bowl, he or she is the winner. If not, the player who tossed the most beans into the bowl is the winner.

8. Continue the game with each group of three players until everyone has had a turn.

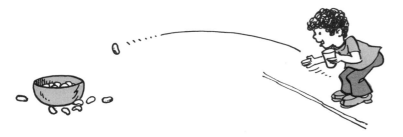

LYNX AND CAT (South Africa)

You need: chalk
yardstick
six medium-sized cartons

Steps:

1. Explain that Bushmen in South Africa understand the behavior of lynxes and cats. They enjoy acting out the animal parts as they play this game of chase.

2. Chalk off a 25' square in an open play area.

3. Place the cartons randomly within the square.

4. Divide the players into two teams. One will be the cats and the other will be the lynxes. Each team stands in a line on opposite sides of the square just behind the chalked line. If there is an uneven number of players, allow one child to take two turns.

5. Let the first child from each team take one step forward. As soon as the player from the cat team says, "Try to catch me," he or she will run anywhere within the chalked area as the lynx chases him or her. The rest of the players clap as they count from one to twenty. The players may run around and between the cartons, but they may not touch them.

6. At the count of "twenty," the chase ends. If the cat has not been caught by the lynx, they each return to their teams. If the cat is caught by the lynx, the cat must join the lynx's team. Then the next set of players steps forward to take a turn.

7. Each set of players plays the game in the same manner described in steps 5 and 6.

8. After all the lynxes have chased all the cats, the players count the number of cats captured by the lynxes. The teams exchange roles, and play continues until each set of players has had a turn to play the opposite role. The players again count the number of cats captured.

9. The winning team is the one that captures more cats.

EGYPTIAN FESTIVAL OF SPRING BREEZES
Worksheet

At the beginning of spring, children in Egypt celebrate the Festival of Spring Breezes. To find out what children do on this day, solve the problems in the lettered boxes at the right. Then fill in each numbered space at the bottom of this page with the letter from the matching box.

Name_____

A 12 +24	T 14 +23	C 13 +25
H 14 +25	N 18 +10	V 16 +13
I 15 +10	E 11 +10	P 14 +32
Y 12 +37		

___ ___ ___ ___   ___ ___ ___ ___
37 39 21 49   39 36 29 21

___   ___ ___ ___ ___ ___ ___ .
36   46 25 38 28 25 38

YAM FESTIVAL
West African Art Activity / Recipe

The Yam Festival is celebrated in West Africa at harvesttime every August. Children enjoy picnics, play games, and make good luck Akuaba dolls. Have your class make Akuaba doll pendants, following the steps on this page. Then have children help prepare the yam recipe on this page.

AKUABA DOLL PENDANTS

You need: cutouts on page 36
crayons or markers
scissors
ruler
pencil
glue
oaktag
brightly colored yarn
drinking straws
clear tape

Steps:

1. Reproduce the Akuaba doll cutouts on page 36 for each child.

2. Have each child color one of the two cutouts and cut it out along the dotted lines.

3. Measure and cut a 3″ × 6″ piece of oaktag for each child.

4. Let each child glue the blank side of the cutout onto the oaktag.

5. Have children cut their oaktag pieces into three sections, along the solid lines.

6. Measure and cut a 30″ piece of yarn for each child. Apply a small amount of glue to one end of the yarn and let it harden. Help children thread the glued ends through the straws and knot them three times.

7. Have each child tape the threaded straw to the back of the three cutout sections, leaving approximately ¼″ space between the sections. See illustration.

8. Make a loop with the unglued end of the yarn and help children knot it securely just above the straw. Children can then wear their Akuaba pendants hung around their necks.

STEP 7.

FU FU

Ingredients: three or four yams
water
½ teaspoon salt
⅛ teaspoon pepper

Optional: 3 tablespoons honey or sugar

How to Make:

1. Wash and peel yams. Cut into ½″ slices.

2. Place slices in a large saucepan and add water to cover them.

3. Bring to a boil over a hot plate or stove.

4. Reduce heat, cover saucepan, and simmer for 20 to 25 minutes, until yams are soft enough to mash.

5. Remove saucepan from stove and drain off liquid into a small bowl. Let yams cool for 15 minutes.

6. Place yam slices in a medium-sized mixing bowl, mash with a fork, add salt and pepper, and mash again till smooth.

7. Roll mixture into small, walnut-sized balls. If mixture is too dry, moisten it with a tablespoon of the reserved yam liquid.

8. For sweeter Fu Fu, roll yam balls in a dish of honey or sugar. (Makes 24 balls.)

YAM FESTIVAL
Cutouts

Distribute copies of this page to your class and discuss the animals listed below. These animals are commonly found in Australia. Then reproduce the worksheet on page 38 for children to complete.

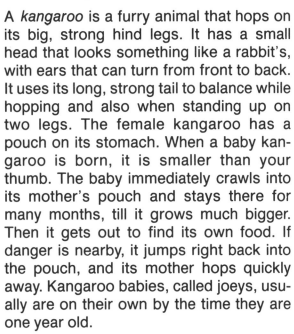

kangaroo

koala

A *kangaroo* is a furry animal that hops on its big, strong hind legs. It has a small head that looks something like a rabbit's, with ears that can turn from front to back. It uses its long, strong tail to balance while hopping and also when standing up on two legs. The female kangaroo has a pouch on its stomach. When a baby kangaroo is born, it is smaller than your thumb. The baby immediately crawls into its mother's pouch and stays there for many months, till it grows much bigger. Then it gets out to find its own food. If danger is nearby, it jumps right back into the pouch, and its mother hops quickly away. Kangaroo babies, called joeys, usually are on their own by the time they are one year old.

The *koala* spends almost all of its time in trees, and only comes down to move to other ones. Its long toes and sharp, curved claws help it hang onto the branches. Koalas sleep most of the day and stay awake during the night. Many people think a koala looks like a bear, with its soft thick fur, round bushy ears, and big black nose. Koalas, though, are not related to bears. Female koalas have pouches like kangaroos, and their tiny babies stay in them for many months. They then come out and ride on their mothers' backs for about six months before they learn to live on their own.

An *emu* is a bird that is as big as a man. It has very tiny wings, though, and cannot fly. Its legs are long and strong, so it is a very good runner. It is also an excellent swimmer. The female emu lays eight to ten green eggs at a time. She places them in a cozy nest of leaves and grass. Then the father emu sits on the eggs until they hatch. An emu likes to eat caterpillars, leaves, and fruit. It is the national bird of Australia.

The *dingo* is a wild dog that lives in Australia. Only its toes and the tip of its tail are white. It does not bark, but makes a howling sound instead. If you want to make a pet of a dingo, you must capture it when it is a puppy. Otherwise, it will not be friendly. Dingoes sometimes live in dens among the rocks, in large holes underground, or inside the hollow parts of trees.

Each morning and each evening, people in some parts of Australia can hear the loud sound of the *kookaburra*, a large bird that lives in the forest. It sits on the branch of a tree and makes a strange noise that sounds like laughter. Kookaburras do not build nests but live in holes inside the trees instead. The kookaburra likes to eat frogs, snakes, insects, caterpillars, worms, and other very small birds. It has a long bill and black, brown, and white feathers.

emu

dingo

kookaburra

Name_____

Look at the pictures of animals found in Australia, in the boxes at the bottom of the page. Color the pictures. Then cut out each box along the dotted lines and paste it onto the matching box in the scene below. Color the rest of the scene.

kangaroo dingo kookaburra emu koala

SWEDISH PANCAKES

Ingredients: three eggs
1 cup milk
1½ cups flour
1 tablespoon sugar
½ teaspoon salt
4 tablespoons butter
1 cup heavy cream
2 tablespoons confectioner's sugar or
12-oz. jar of fruit jelly

How to Make:

1. Using a fork or whisk, beat the eggs lightly in a large mixing bowl.

2. Add half the milk.

3. Fold in the flour, sugar, and salt.

4. Melt the butter and add it, the cream, and the remaining milk to the mixture. Stir well.

5. Lightly grease a frying pan or griddle, and place it over medium-high heat on a hot plate or stove.

6. Carefully pour small amounts of the mixture onto the frying pan or griddle. Cook until the pancakes are golden around the edges and bubbly on top. Turn the pancakes over with a spatula and cook until the other sides are golden around the edges.

7. Remove to a covered plate. Repeat step 6 until all the mixture is used up.

8. Sprinkle pancakes lightly with confectioner's sugar, or spread fruit jelly over them. (Makes three dozen pancakes.)

FINNISH STRAWBERRY SHAKE

Ingredients: 20 fresh strawberries
4 cups milk
3 tablespoons sugar

How to Make:

1. Wash strawberries and cut off stems.

2. Cut strawberries into small pieces.

3. Combine milk, sugar, and strawberries in a large mixing bowl.

4. Beat with an eggbeater for two minutes.

5. Pour the strawberry shakes into individual glasses. (Makes four servings.)

Variation:

Raspberries or other sweet berries may be used instead.

HOLIDAY HEART BASKETS

You need: several 6″ paper plates
pencils
9″ × 12″ red and green construction paper
scissors
glue
small doilies
ruler

Step 2

Steps:

1. Have each child trace a 6″ paper plate once onto red construction paper and once onto green construction paper. Have children cut out their circles.

2. Ask each child to fold the circles in half and place the rounded side of one folded circle inside the other so that the folded ends meet at the bottom and flare out at the top. This will form a heart shape. (See illustration.) Glue the inside halves of the circles to the outside halves.

3. Next each child cuts a doily in half. He or she spreads glue on one side of both halves and presses them inside the basket so that the doily shows above the basket rim as in illustration.

4. Cut ½″ × 6″ strips of red construction paper to make handles for the baskets. Have each child glue the two ends of a strip onto opposite top edges of the basket, as shown.

5. Prepare the gingersnap recipe on this page with your class and fill the children's baskets with these traditional Christmas cookies.

GINGERSNAPS

Ingredients: ¼ cup butter
1 cup sugar
one egg
1 teaspoon vinegar
¼ cup molasses
2 cups flour
1 to 2 teaspoons ginger
¾ teaspoon baking soda
¼ teaspoon cinnamon
30 marshmallows

How to Make:

1. Preheat oven to 325° F.

2. Cream the butter and sugar together.

3. Stir in the egg, vinegar, and molasses.

4. Sift and add the flour.

5. Add the ginger, baking soda, and cinnamon. Mix all the ingredients until blended.

6. Form the dough into quarter-sized balls, and bake on a greased cookie sheet for 8 minutes.

7. Remove the cookies and add half a marshmallow, cut side down, to the top of each cookie.

8. Return cookies to the oven for 4 minutes. (Makes five dozen cookies.)

NEW YEAR'S IN THE BRITISH ISLES
Recipes

Each country has a unique way of celebrating the New Year. In Scotland, a special sun-shaped shortbread is eaten. In England, everyone enjoys a delicious drink of wassail, a fruity punch. Celebrate New Year's Day in your class by having children help prepare and serve the recipes on this page.

SCOTTISH SHORTBREAD

Ingredients: ½ cup confectioner's sugar
1 cup softened sweet butter or margarine
2 cups flour

How to Make:

1. Preheat oven to 325° F.

2. Mix the sugar and butter or margarine together in a large bowl with a fork.

3. Add flour and mix until blended. Shape the dough into a ball and chill it slightly.

4. Place dough on a greased cookie sheet.

5. Gently roll dough into a 10″ circle about ½″ thick.

6. Use a knife to cut 16 small triangles from around the edge of the shortbread, to give it a sun shape. See illustration.

7. Use a fork to prick eight radial dotted lines into the shortbread to make eight equal wedges. See illustration.

8. Bake the shortbread for 45 minutes, or until golden brown. Cool and serve. (Makes eight large wedges of shortbread.)

Step 6

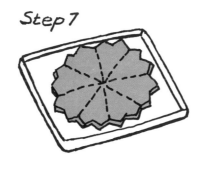
Step 7

ENGLISH WASSAIL

Explain to children that traditionally the different colored fruits in wassail bring different fortunes for the new year. Red apple means wealth, green grapes mean happiness, an orange slice means a surprise, and a yellow lemon means something funny to come.

Ingredients: 1 liter ginger ale
1 liter orange juice
1 liter pineapple juice
one orange
one lemon
one apple
ten seedless green grapes

How to Make:

1. Into a large bowl pour the ginger ale and juices. Stir.

2. Slice the orange and lemon into six to eight pieces each and add to the wassail.

3. Cut the apple in half and core it. Slice the halves into three pieces each. Add the apple slices and grapes to the wassail.

4. Using a ladle, serve in 7-oz. paper cups. Have children discover their fortunes from the fruit they receive in their wassail. (Makes 24 four-ounce servings.)

Children in Italy go to Christmas fairs and markets where they can buy Befana dolls for the holiday of Epiphany. Befana is a little old woman, similar to Santa Claus, who brings gifts to children. Make Befana dolls in your class using the instructions and pattern below.

You need: one toilet paper tube for each child
ruler
pencils
scissors
light-colored construction paper
glue
fine-line markers
arms pattern on this page
oaktag
green, yellow, and red crepe paper
drinking straws
transparent tape

Steps:

1. Give each child a toilet paper tube.

2. Measure and cut a 4½" × 7" piece of construction paper for each child.

3. Have each child spread glue on one side of the construction paper and wind it, glue-side down, around the tube.

4. Using fine-line markers, each child will draw Befano's face on the top third of the tube.

5. Reproduce the arms pattern. Cut it out and trace it several times onto oaktag. Cut the patterns out and have each child trace one onto construction paper. Then each child will cut out the Befana doll's arms.

6. Help each child glue the center of the arms pattern to the back of the doll, starting from just under the place where a neck would be. Fold the unglued part where indicated by the dotted lines to make elbows.

7. Measure and cut a 2½" × 7" piece of green crepe paper for each child. This will be Befana's skirt. Each child will spread glue on the tube, starting from under the arms. Making sure the seam is at the back, have children glue the crepe paper to the tube. Pull out the bottom of the crepe paper to widen the skirt.

8. For Befana's apron, measure and cut a 2" × 2½" piece of yellow crepe paper for each child. Have children glue the apron onto the front of the skirt.

9. For Befana's kerchief, measure and cut 3½" × 12" strips of red crepe paper. Help each child to center a strip on Befana's head. Fold over a fraction of an inch to cover the forehead. Place a dot of glue under the crepe paper and press. Then pull the ends forward, tie them in front of Befana's apron, and glue the kerchief to the tube. See illustration.

10. For Befana's broom, measure and cut straws into 3½" lengths. Split the ends of each up to 1". Tape the broom handle onto one of Befana's hands.

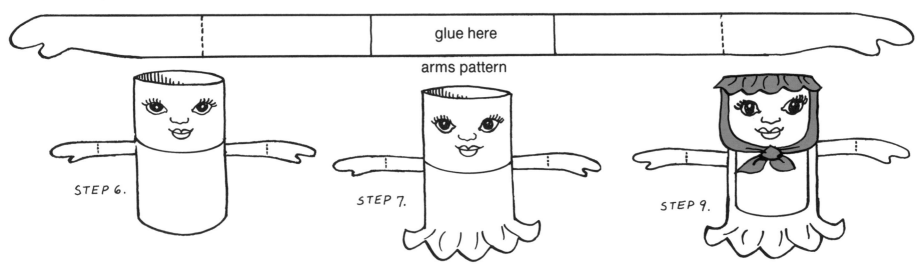

glue here

arms pattern

STEP 6.   STEP 7.   STEP 9.

BUDULINEK
Czech Folktale

Read the folktale on this page and page 44 to your class. Then reproduce the worksheet on page 45 for children to complete.

Budulinek was a happy little boy who lived with his grandmother in a cottage in the woods. Every morning Granny prepared a hot, tasty meal for Budulinek before she went off to work. And every morning Granny told Budulinek never to open the door while she was away.

One morning, Granny prepared a delicious bowl of soup, kissed Budulinek good-bye, and went off into the woods. No sooner had she left than Budulinek heard a knock on the door. It was Lishka, the fox.

"Let me in, Budulinek. I will give you a ride on my tail," she cried. Budulinek knew he wasn't supposed to let anyone in, but he thought of the fun he would have, and he opened the door. Lishka jumped in, ran right over to the soup, and ate it all up. Then she turned around and ran out of the house. Budulinek was very hungry all day, and by the time Granny returned that evening, Budulinek was sobbing great big tears. Granny scolded Budulinek, reminding him never, never to open the door when she wasn't there. And Budulinek promised to remember for the next time.

The next morning, Granny prepared a big bowl of porridge, with honey on top, for Budulinek. She kissed him good-bye and went off to work. Right after she left, Budulinek heard a knock on the door again. There was Lishka the fox back again.

"Open the door, Budulinek. It's Lishka. Let me in," she called. This time Budulinek didn't open the door.

Then Lishka called again, "I know I fooled you yesterday, but today I really will give you a ride on my tail. You can trust me." Budulinek thought about the wonderful ride he could have.

"This time maybe she really will give me a ride," he said to himself. And so, he opened the door. Lishka came right into the room, gobbled up all the porridge, and ran right out again. Budulinek was left without his food once more. By the time Granny came home, he was very hungry and crying great big tears. Granny was very angry at Budulinek and told him that if he ever opened the door again she would have to spank him.

The next morning Granny prepared a tasty bowl of peas for Budulinek. As soon as she left, Budulinek decided to eat all the peas. Just as he was taking a spoonful, Lishka knocked on the door again. This time Budulinek took his bowl to the window so Lishka could see him eating.

Lishka said, "Let me in, Budulinek. This time I promise you I really, really will give you a ride on my tail."

"No," answered Budulinek, remembering what Granny had told him.

But Lishka kept on begging and begging to come in until Budulinek finally said, "Okay," and opened the door. Lishka immediately snatched the remaining peas from the bowl, gobbled them up, and then, instead of turning to leave, said, "Now, jump on my tail and I'll give you a ride."

Off they went into the forest. Budulinek was so delighted he didn't realize that Lishka was taking him for a ride to her den deep under the ground. She hid Budulinek in the den with her three fox children, who bit him and pinched him. Budulinek was very unhappy.

When Granny came home that evening and found Budulinek missing, she cried and cried. Days went by and Budulinek did not return. Granny grew sadder and sadder.

One day an organ-grinder came by playing a pretty tune. Granny told him about Budulinek, her poor lost grandson.

"Don't worry, Granny," said the organ-grinder. "I'll find him. I have a plan."

With that, the organ-grinder left and continued on his way through the woods. Soon he heard the distant sound of a boy crying, and as he came closer to Lishka's den, the sound became louder and louder. The organ-grinder began to play his music. Soon Lishka's oldest fox child came out to see from where the music was coming. The organ-grinder caught the little fox and stuffed him into his sack. The organ-grinder then began to play again. Out came the other two little foxes to hear the pretty music. Again the organ-grinder caught them and stuffed them into his sack. He then started to play his music again. This time, out came Lishka herself to see what was happening. As quick as a wink, the organ-grinder caught her, too.

Then the organ-grinder called down to Budulinek in the underground den, "Come out, Budulinek. It's all right. Lishka will not stop you." With that, Budulinek came out, and the organ-grinder took him home to Granny. But before that, the organ-grinder punished the foxes by giving them a beating. They promised never again to do anything to Budulinek.

The organ-grinder, Granny, and Budulinek had a wonderful dinner together that evening. The organ-grinder played music while Granny rocked in her rocking chair. Budulinek thought about Lishka the fox and he never opened the door when he was alone again.

Discussion Questions:

1. What did Granny tell Budulinek never to do?
2. Who knocked on the door when Granny was gone?
3. What did Budulinek do each time?
4. What did Lishka do on the third morning?
5. Who helped Budulinek escape from the foxes?
6. How did Budulinek finally get back home to Granny?

BUDULINEK
Maze Worksheet

Name_____

Help the organ-grinder find Budulinek.
Trace the organ-grinder's path to the fox's den.
Do not cross any lines.

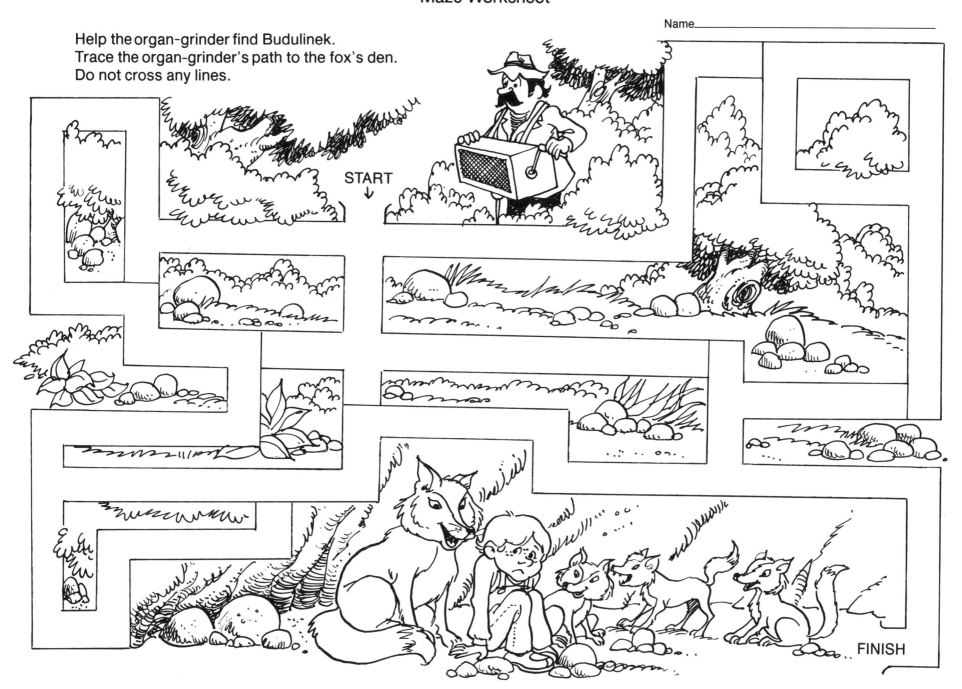

START

FINISH

LONG MAY YOU LIVE
Dutch Birthday Song

On the morning of a Dutch child's birthday, the entire family sings this song to him or her. A chair is specially decorated with flowers and streamers for the child. He or she brings cookies or candies to school for classmates but does not receive any presents.

Long may you live, ___ long may you live, ___ Long may you live ___ in hap - pi - ness, In ___ hap - pi - ness, in ___ hap - pi - ness.

You need: chair
streamers
flowers, real or artificial
string

Steps:

1. Teach children the song.

2. When children become familiar with it, teach them the Dutch words included on this page.

3. At the beginning of each month, have children whose birthdays are in that month decorate a chair by entwining streamers and tying flowers with string around the back of it.

4. Whenever a child has a birthday, have children sit in a circle. Place the decorated chair in the center of the circle.

5. During the school year, on the day of each child's birthday, he or she will sit on the chair as the rest of the class sings the song to him or her.

6. At the end of the school year, have all children with summer birthdays take turns sitting on the decorated chair as the rest of the class sings to them.

Dutch Verse

Lang zal die leven
Lang zal die leven
Lang zal die leven in de gloria
In de gloria, in de gloria.

Steps:

1. Explain to children that in Poland *tah-toosh* is an affectionate term for "father," similar to "daddy" in the United States.

2. Teach children the song "Tah-Toosh and I." Ask all the children to stand in a circle, facing the center, as they sing the song.

3. As the children sing each verse, have them dramatize the activity mentioned for each particular day of the week, as suggested on this page.

4. After singing the song, reproduce the worksheet on page 48 for each child.

On a Mon - day morn - ing, shi - ny Mon - day morn - ing,
Sow - ing seeds, Tah - toosh and I, sow - ing when the sun was high.
Sow - ing seeds, Tah - toosh and I, Sow - ing when the sun was high.

On a Monday morning,
   shiny Monday morning,
Sowing seeds, Tah-toosh and I,
Sowing when the sun was high.
Sowing seeds, Tah-toosh and I,
Sowing when the sun was high.

(Sprinkle imaginary seeds on the ground.)

On a Tuesday morning,
   shiny Tuesday morning,
Mowing hay, Tah-toosh and I,
Mowing when the sun was high.
Mowing hay, Tah-toosh and I,
Mowing when the sun was high.

(Swing arms back and forth in front of you.)

On a Wednesday morning,
   shiny Wednesday morning,
Drying hay, Tah-toosh and I,
Drying when the sun was high.
Drying hay, Tah-toosh and I,
Drying when the sun was high.

(Scoop up imaginary hay in your arms and toss it upward.)

On a Thursday morning,
   shiny Thursday morning,
Raking hay, Tah-toosh and I,
Raking when the sun was high.
Raking hay, Tah-toosh and I
Raking when the sun was high.

(Make raking motions with your arms.)

On a Friday morning,
   shiny Friday morning,
Stacking hay, Tah-toosh and I,
Stacking when the sun was high.
Stacking hay, Tah-toosh and I,
Stacking when the sun was high.

(Bend to pick up imaginary hay and place it in a pile that grows higher and higher.)

On a Saturday morning,
   shiny Saturday morning,
Selling hay, Tah-toosh and I,
Selling when the sun was high.
Selling hay, Tah-toosh and I,
Selling when the sun was high.

(Hold an imaginary bale of hay in both hands. Pretend to give it to the child next to you.)

On a Sunday morning,
   shiny Sunday morning,
Rest all day, Tah-toosh and I,
Resting when the sun was high.
Rest all day, Tah-toosh and I,
Resting when the sun was high.

(Close eyes, put hands on cheek, and rock from side to side.)

Name_____

After you have learned the song "Tah-Toosh and I," color the pictures
on this page.
Cut them out along the dotted lines.
Paste the pictures in the right order onto a long strip of paper.

KICK THE STICK (Norway)

You need: chalk
two flat rocks or two wooden blocks
  of the same height
18″ – 24″ stick
small markers, such as stones,
  bottle caps, paper clips,
  for each player

Steps:

1. Explain that this game is played by Norwegian children at the first sign of spring.

2. Use chalk to draw a starting line at one end of a play area.

3. Place the rocks or blocks 6′ beyond the starting line, just far enough apart from each other so that the stick can be balanced across them.

4. Let groups of four to six children play this game. Give each player a different marker.

5. Each child, in turn, runs from the starting line to the balanced stick and kicks it as far as he or she can. The player then places his or her marker on that spot to indicate where the stick has landed. After each child's turn, balance the stick across the rocks or blocks again.

6. Give three points to the child whose marker is farthest from the starting line, two points to the child with the next farthest marker, and one point to the child with the third farthest marker.

7. Play the game for three rounds. The child with the highest cumulative score is the winner.

Variation:

For older children, place the balanced stick farther away from the starting line and have children play five or six rounds.

THIRD PERSON OUT (Denmark)

You need: chalk

Steps:

1. Use the chalk to draw a 20′ circle on the ground.

2. Choose one player to be the runner and another player to be "it." The runner stands in the center of the circle. The child who is "it" stands anywhere within the circle. Divide all the other players into couples, who stand one in front of the other along the inside of the circle, facing the center. If there is an uneven number of players, have one child be the caller.

3. Players must remain inside the chalked circle throughout the game. When the caller shouts "One, two, three—third person out!" "it" chases the runner in order to tag him or her.

4. The runner tries to avoid being tagged by running to any couple, and standing behind the children to create a threesome. The player in the front becomes the new runner. "It" chases the new runner.

5. If "it" tags a runner, they change roles, so that the tagged runner now becomes the new "it" and the previous "it" becomes the runner. Select another child to be the new caller, if necessary.

6. The game continues for as long as time allows and interest is sustained.

Variation:

Once a runner is tagged, the teacher can select two new players to be the runner and "it." The previous runner and "it" can then join the circle and become another couple.

THE DONKEY AND THE HEN
Italian Rounds

Italian children enjoy these songs in which they imitate barnyard animals and sing in two groups.

L'ASINO (The Donkey)

Now that the sun's up the don - key starts to sing.

Who sings the loud - est shall be the don - key king!

Rah! Rah! Rah, rah, rah!

Steps:

1. Teach children each song, one line at a time.

2. When children are familiar with the words, divide the class into two groups to sing each song as a round.

3. For each song, have the first group of children begin to sing. As they start to sing the fifth measure, the second group will begin to sing. (For "L'Asino," the fifth measure begins with the word "Who." For "La Gallina," the fifth measure begins with the word "Announcing.")

4. Have children sing each song twice through. As the second group reaches the last word of each song, let all the children make the sound of the animal.

LA GALLINA (The Hen)

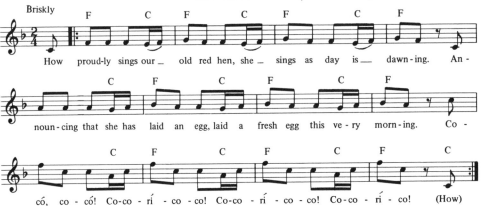

How proud-ly sings our _ old red hen, she _ sings as day is _ dawn-ing. An -

noun-cing that she has laid an egg, laid a fresh egg this ve-ry morn-ing. Co -

có, co - có! Co-co - rí - co-co! Co-co - rí - co-co! Co-co - rí - co! (How)

Read the story on this page and page 52 to your class. Then have children do the suggested follow-up activity.

There was once a poor miller who owned only a mill, a donkey, and a cat. When the miller died, he left the mill to his oldest son, the donkey to his middle son, and the cat to his youngest son.

The youngest son was very unhappy. "What use is a cat to me?" he wondered. "A cat can't help me earn a living."

"Don't worry, master," said the cat, whose name was Puss. "If you give me a bag and a pair of boots, I will make sure you live very well."

So the young man gave Puss what he asked for. Puss pulled on his boots, took the bag, and tramped off into a field to hunt. He laid the bag down and put some lettuce inside it. Then he lay down beside the bag and pretended to sleep. Before long a rabbit hopped into the bag to nibble on the lettuce. Quick as a wink, Puss closed the bag and carried the rabbit off to the king's palace.

When Puss stood before the king, he bowed low and said, "Your Majesty, my master asked me to bring you this rabbit as a present."

"Who is your master?" asked the king. Puss quickly invented an important-sounding name for his master.

"The Marquis of Carabas," answered Puss.

"Tell him I thank him for his present," said the king. Puss bowed again and left. Every day from then on, Puss brought a rabbit for the king.

One day Puss learned that the king and his beautiful daughter planned to take a carriage ride along the river. Puss told his master, "I have a plan. Do as I say, and you shall become the happiest man in the kingdom. Now take your clothes off and go for a swim in the river."

And the young man did. Puss hid his master's clothes under a large stone and waited. When he saw the king's carriage driving by, Puss ran up to it and shouted, "Help! My master, the Marquis of Carabas, is drowning!"

The king stopped his carriage and ordered his men to rescue the marquis. As his master was pulled from the river, Puss told the king, "While my master was swimming, a robber stole his clothes." So the king commanded his servant to hurry and bring a fine suit of clothes for the marquis. When he put on the clothes, the young man looked very handsome.

"Come take a ride with us, Marquis," said the king. And the marquis climbed into the carriage and sat next to the princess.

Puss walked ahead of the carriage. When he came to a field where some workers were picking corn, Puss said, "When the king drives by, you must tell him that all this corn belongs to the Marquis of Carabas. If you do not, you will be chopped into tiny pieces." The workers were very afraid. When the king called out to them, "Whose corn is this?" the workers answered, "All this corn belongs to the Marquis of Carabas."

"What fine land you own, Marquis," said the king as they drove on.

Puss tramped on ahead of the carriage until he came to a lovely castle where a rich and mighty ogre lived. The ogre owned all the land around the castle, including the cornfield the king had admired. Bravely Puss went to the castle gate and asked to see the ogre.

"Mighty ogre, I have heard of your magical powers," said Puss. "Tell me, is it true that you can change yourself into a lion?"

"Of course I can," replied the ogre proudly. "Just watch." And suddenly a huge lion stood before Puss. He was so terrified that he jumped onto the windowsill. After a moment the ogre changed back into his usual self and Puss came down from the windowsill.

"That was wonderful," said Puss. "I have also heard that you can turn yourself into a very tiny creature, but that must be impossible. You are too big to become a tiny mouse, for example."

"Ha! I can change myself into a mouse very easily," bragged the ogre, and he did. As soon as Puss saw the little mouse, he pounced on it and ate it up.

Just then the king's carriage pulled up in front of the castle. Puss ran out and greeted the king, saying, "Welcome to the castle of the Marquis of Carabas, Your Majesty." Then he led the king, his daughter, and the marquis into the dining hall where a marvelous feast was set on the great table.

"Marquis, your castle and lands are magnificent," said the king, "and you are a noble young man. It would please me very much if you would marry my daughter." The marquis bowed very low and said, "Nothing would make me happier, Your Majesty."

That very day the marquis and the princess were married. The marquis rewarded Puss by giving him great riches.

Follow-up Activity:

Let each child draw his or her favorite scene from the story on a piece of 12″ × 18″ white construction paper. Have each child write or dictate a sentence telling about his or her drawing, to go at the bottom of the picture. Then post the children's drawings on a bulletin board.

HA-HA, THIS-A-WAY
American Song / Game

When I was a young child, young child, young child, When I was a young child, then, oh then.

Ha - ha, this-a-way, ha - ha, that-a-way, Ha - ha, this-a-way, then, oh then.

Steps:

1. Teach children the verses and chorus of "Ha-Ha, This-A-Way."

2. Have children stand in a circle. Select one child to be the leader and have that child stand in the center of the circle.

3. As the children sing each verse, the leader will perform an action appropriate for the character named in the verse. The leader can use movements such as walking, skipping, marching, or hopping.

4. As the children sing the chorus, they move around in the circle imitating the actions of the leader.

5. Select a new leader for each of the verses listed below.

Verse 2

When I was a cowboy(cowgirl), cowboy(cowgirl), cowboy(cowgirl),
When I was a cowboy(cowgirl), then, oh then.
(chorus)

Verse 3

When I was a soldier, soldier, soldier,
When I was a soldier, then, oh then.
(chorus)

Verse 4

When I was a dancer, dancer, dancer,
When I was a dancer, then, oh then.
(chorus)

Verse 5

When I was an old man(woman), old man(woman), old man(woman),
When I was an old man(woman), then, oh then.
(chorus)

Variation:

Encourage children to make up their own verses and to give suggestions for acting them out. Add these verses to the rest when playing "Ha-Ha, This-A-Way."

YUMMY DESSERTS
Brazilian Recipes

Cocadas and brigadeiros are sold in busy shopping areas by "Bahianas," women from Bahia. They dress in colorful blouses, long skirts, hoop earrings, and beaded necklaces. After preparing the recipes, have children complete the worksheet on page 55.

COCADAS

Ingredients: 1 cup sugar
¼ cup water
1 cup shredded coconut

How to Make:

1. Mix the sugar and water in a saucepan, and cook over medium heat on a hot plate or stove.

2. Stir constantly with a wooden spoon until mixture reaches the consistency of a soft ball. (To test, drop some of the mixture into a cup of water. When removed, it will form a soft ball that does not hold its shape but flattens when held.)

3. Remove from heat. Beat the mixture with a spoon for 30 seconds.

4. Add coconut to the mixture and beat for another 30 seconds.

5. Spoon walnut-sized portions of the mixture onto a large plate.

6. Allow to cool before serving. (Makes 12 cocadas.)

BRIGADEIROS

Ingredients: 4-oz. semisweet chocolate
one 14-oz. can sweetened condensed milk
¼ cup butter
one egg
small box chocolate sprinkles

How to Make:

1. Melt the chocolate in a saucepan over low heat.

2. Add the next three ingredients, mix together using a wooden spoon, and cook over low heat.

3. Keep stirring the mixture until it is thick enough to leave the side of the pan. (This may take as long as 30 minutes.)

4. Remove mixture from heat and cool. Then have children form marble-sized balls of brigadeiros and roll each in chocolate sprinkles. (Makes 25 brigadeiros.)

Bahia is a large city in Brazil.
The women from Bahia wear colorful costumes.
Look at the pictures below.
Find the two women who look exactly the same.
Circle them and color their costumes exactly the same.
Then color the rest of the pictures.

Name_____

Read the story of "The Wildcat and the Frog" to your class and ask children the discussion questions that follow. Then have the children complete the worksheet on page 57.

One sunny morning Frog was sitting by the pond, as still as a rock, when Wildcat came by to get a drink of water.

"Good morning, Wildcat! How are you this fine day?" asked Frog politely.

"What?" snarled Wildcat. "How dare you talk to me! You are so small and ugly and weak. Move away from this spot by the pond so I can drink in peace."

"Now just a minute, Wildcat," said Frog calmly. "This pond is my home, and you are behaving very rudely. It may be true that I am ugly and weak, but I am brave, too."

"How can such a little fellow as you be brave?" sneered Wildcat. "I don't believe you at all."

"Well, I'll show you how brave I am," answered Frog. "First you roar and then I'll croak. We'll see which one of us becomes more frightened." Wildcat laughed loudly when he heard Frog's plan.

"You are a very foolish frog. It won't take much for me to frighten you," said Wildcat. He took a great big breath and let out a long, ferocious roar that thundered through the forest. All the other animals were so terrified that they ran and hid. Only Frog stayed, very calm and very still.

"It's your turn now, Frog. Let me hear you croak!" said Wildcat.

Frog closed his eyes and took such a deep breath that he seemed to puff up to twice his size. In a moment he opened his mouth and began a long, low, soft croak. All of a sudden, from all over the pond, all of Frog's friends and relatives started to croak along with him. Together they made one big loud C-R-R-R-R-R-O-A-K that echoed right through the forest and made the leaves tremble on their branches.

Wildcat was caught by surprise. He got such a fright that he jumped right up, put his tail between his legs, and ran as fast as he could away from the pond. To this day he is still running.

Discussion Questions:

1. Where was Frog sitting?

2. Who came by?

3. Why was Wildcat mean to Frog?

4. What did Frog do to show he was brave?

5. What happened when Frog began to croak?

6. Who was braver, Wildcat or Frog? Why do you think so?

Look at the picture below to find the hiding frogs.
Circle each frog and color the frogs green.
Then color the rest of the picture.
How many frogs are hiding in the picture?_____

Name_____

Come on and join in this song, this song,

Sing out and clap right a - long, a - long!

Dance in a cir - cle this way, this way,

It's Chia - pa - ne - cas, o - lé!

Verse 2:

Oh, Chiapanecas, hey, hey! (clap, clap)
Oh, Chiapanecas, hey, hey! (clap, clap)
Oh, Chiapanecas, hey, hey! (clap, clap)
Oh, Chiapanecas, olé! Olé!

Steps:

1. Teach children both verses of the song, one line at a time.

2. When children are familiar with the words, have them stand in a circle. Explain that in the second verse, they will clap twice each time they finish singing the words "hey, hey!"

3. Next have children march around in the circle as they sing. They will stop marching and clap, after the words "hey, hey!" and then continue to sing and march again. At the end of the song children will shout the second "Olé!" and clap loudly.

Follow-up Activity:

Distribute a rhythm instrument to each of four children. You can use a triangle, set of wood blocks, set of sticks, pair of bells, tambourine, maracas, drum, or set of sand blocks. Select two of these children to play their instruments during the first two lines of the song in time to the music, while the rest of the class sings. They will be followed by the other two children, who will play during the next two lines of the song, while the rest of the class sings. The four children repeat their performance for the second verse of the song. On the last word of the song, all four children will play their rhythm instruments together as the rest of the class shouts out "Olé!"

Read this story to your class and ask children the discussion questions that follow.

In the middle of a pond close to Lake Managua, there lived a frog who could swim faster, jump higher, and croak louder than any of his friends and relatives. He was quite pleased with himself until, one long winter season while he was sleeping, he dreamed he could fly.

When he woke up the next spring he wanted to fly, but found he couldn't. He tried anyway, flapping his front legs quickly while leaping up higher and higher on his hind legs. That didn't help at all.

Finally, when two large, gray ducks landed on the pond on their way north, he had an idea.

"Noble ducks," he called, as he swam close to them, "I had a wonderful dream last winter, and you would make me very happy if you could make it come true."

"Tell us how, friend Frog," said the ducks.

"I dreamed I could fly through the air," said the frog. "Now I find that I can't. But if each of you can hold opposite ends of a strong reed in your bills, I will hold the center of it in my mouth. If I flap my legs as you swoop through the air, I will be able to fly."

"That's true," said the two ducks. "We will gladly help you. But remember, don't speak to us or call out when we're flying, or you'll take a nasty fall."

So the frog found a reed, and soon all three of them were swooping through the air, while the other frogs clapped and cheered from the pond below. The birds sang merrily in the trees, and all the animals came out of the forest to watch in wonder.

Soon the frog became so confident and excited he began doing tricks. First he clapped his hind legs together. Then he held onto the reed with his front feet. He even turned somersaults in the air, letting go of the reed as he flipped backward, and then catching onto the reed again with his mouth. The ducks also became excited and began performing tricks. They flew around in circles, they looped the loop, they turned, and they swooped down from high in the air.

At last they dove so steeply that the frog became frightened to see what looked like the pond coming up swiftly toward him. "Stop, please stop!" he cried.

But as he called out, he had to let go of the reed. Splash! He fell straight into the pond. Dozens of frogs jumped in panic to get out of his way. Down he went into the water — down, down, down, until he could finally turn around and swim back up.

"What happened?" asked his friends when at last he puffed his way to the surface.

"I don't want to talk about it," said the frog, feeling foolish. And he still refuses to talk about it, to this day.

Discussion Questions:

1. What was it that the frog dreamed he could do?

2. What did the frog plan to do to be able to fly?

3. What happened to the frog when he called to the ducks to stop their tricks?

4. Why didn't the frog want to talk about his flying?

Hold a Puerto Rican minifestival with your class. Teach children the song below. Then have children help prepare the recipe on this page.

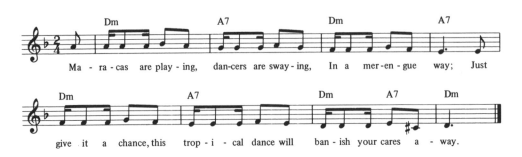

Ma - ra - cas are play - ing, dan-cers are sway - ing, In a mer - en - gue way; Just give it a chance, this trop - i - cal dance will ban - ish your cares a - way.

THE MERENGUE

You need: maracas
rhythm sticks

Optional: castanets

Steps:

1. Have children listen as you sing the song.

2. Teach children the words to the song, one line at a time.

3. When children are familiar with the words, distribute the maracas and rhythm sticks to individual children. Older children can use castanets. Allow children to play the instruments to the beat of the music, while the rest of the class sings the song.

Variation:

Teach the children a simple merengue dance step. The children stand in a circle facing the center. Each child takes a small step to the left and then slides his or her right foot to meet the left foot. Children will take eight complete merengue steps during the song.

FROZEN FRUIT POPS

Ingredients: 1 cup sugar
2 cups water
three oranges
three lemons
two ripe bananas

How to Make:

1. Mix sugar and water in a medium-sized saucepan and place over medium heat. Cook, stirring all the time, until the sugar dissolves.

2. Remove the pan from heat and let the mixture cool.

3. Cut the oranges and lemons in half. Squeeze the juice from them into a small bowl.

4. Peel the bananas, place them in a large mixing bowl, and mash them with a fork.

5. Add the orange and lemon juice to the mashed bananas and mix.

6. Pour the sugar and water mixture into the mixing bowl and mix.

7. Pour the mixture into an ice cube tray with dividers and place it in the freezer. (The mixture can also be poured into paper cups and frozen.)

8. After 30 minutes, place an ice-cream stick in each section of the ice cube tray and return the tray to the freezer until the fruit pops are frozen (about 2 hours). (Makes 12 fruit pops.)

The scene below shows some things you might see in this mystery country.
Find all six of the letters hidden in the picture and circle them.
On the lines at the bottom of the page, write the letters
from left to right to spell the name of this country.
Then color the picture.

Name_____

In the southwestern United States, Pueblo Indians made woven "squash blossoms" to encourage their crops to grow. Indians in Mexico made a similar woven design that they called a "god's eye" and used as a good-luck symbol.

You need: two craft sticks for each child
glue
scissors
yardstick
medium-weight yarn in various colors
large paper clips

STEP 1

Steps:

1. Ask each child to cross two craft sticks to make an **X** and glue them together, as shown. Let dry. Make a pair of crossed sticks for yourself.

2. Cut several 36" lengths of various colors of yarn for each child. Help each child knot one end of a piece of yarn firmly around the center of the crossed sticks. Do the same with your pair of crossed sticks.

3. Demonstrate how to weave the yarn around the sticks, as follows: Hold the end of one of the crossed sticks, keeping the knot behind the stick and letting the yarn dangle down. Bring the yarn up through the space between two "legs" of the crossed sticks. Wind the yarn once around one of the nearest sticks. Then bring the yarn over the front of the stick to the left of the first stick. Wind the yarn down and around that stick. Then bring the yarn over the front of the stick to the left of that stick and wind the yarn down and around it. Continue winding the yarn in this way, each time bringing the yarn over the front of the stick and then down and around it. You will see a triangular woven pattern after winding the yarn around the sticks several times.

4. Let each child begin weaving a "squash blossom." When a child has used almost all of the first length of yarn, he or she lays the sticks on the desk with the woven design facedown. He or she then knots the end of another length of yarn to the first piece of yarn keeping the knot on the back of the design. Trim the short ends of the yarn near the knot. Assist children if necessary. The child continues working with the new piece of yarn. Additional pieces of yarn of various colors may be attached as needed.

5. When all but about ¾" of the sticks are covered with yarn, wind the free end of the yarn several times around one stick. Trim the yarn and dab a little glue onto the end, pressing it onto the back of the stick to hold it in place.

6. To make a hanger for the squash blossom, bend a large paper clip into an **S** shape. Glue it onto the back of one of the sticks, leaving about half of the clip protruding. Children may take their squash blossoms home as gifts.

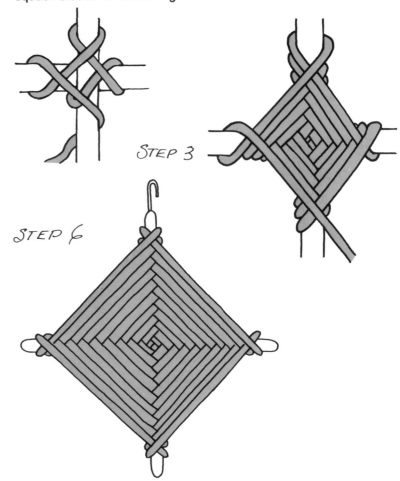

STEP 3

STEP 6

On December 31, in Ecuador, children celebrate the end of the old year just before the new year begins. Families collect old clothes and stuff them with straw or rags to create figures representing the old year. The figures are placed on decorated chairs around which children dance and sing. Everyone writes resolutions and pins them onto the figures. At midnight the figures are removed so the new year can begin with happiness and prosperity. Celebrate the end of the old year with your class by making a stuffed figure as described below. Then pin children's resolutions to it and recite the poem.

You need: old, child-sized, long-sleeved shirt, trousers, scarf, shoes or sneakers, and hat
newspaper or rags
small paper grocery bag (bottom approximately 4½″ × 7½″)
string
markers or crayons
safety pins
chair
writing paper
pencils

Optional: accessories, such as mittens, costume jewelry, school bag, or wig.

Steps:

1. Help children stuff newspaper or rags firmly into the shirt and trousers, so that the stuffing extends about 6″ beyond the bottom edges of each article of clothing.

2. Stuff the paper bag firmly so that the stuffing extends about 6″ beyond the edge of the bag. Tie string around the neck of the bag, one-third of the way from the opening.

3. Hold the bag upside down and draw facial features on it with markers or crayons. Then tuck the stuffing extending from the paper bag into the neck of the shirt. Tie the scarf around the figure's neck.

4. Tuck the stuffing extending from the bottom of the shirt into the top of the figure's trousers. Fasten the shirt and the trousers together with several safety pins.

5. Tuck the stuffing extending from each trouser leg into a shoe or sneaker.

6. Pull out some of the stuffing from each shirt sleeve for a hand. If desired, cover each hand with a mitten.

7. Place the hat on top of the paper bag head. (Allow children to add accessories to the figure, if desired.)

8. Seat the figure on a chair at the front of the room and remind children to handle it with care.

9. Distribute writing paper and a pencil to each child. Have each child write a simple sentence to tell what he or she would like to improve upon or learn about in the new year. (Younger children can dictate their sentences to you.)

10. Use safety pins to attach the papers to the arms, chest, and legs of the figure.

11. Teach children the poem at the bottom of the page to recite as they march in a circle around the "old year" figure.

12. Then read some of the sentences on the figure with the class. Talk about how children can achieve their goals.

> *Good-bye to the old year,*
> *Hello to the new.*
> *There are so many things*
> *I'd like to do.*
> *Next year I'll learn,*
> *And I surely will grow.*
> *Good-bye to the old year,*
> *New year, "Hello!"*

Let children play the games described on this page to strengthen their small motor, visual, and memory skills. In addition, children will become aware of a variety of interesting places around the world.

You need: puzzle boards and puzzle pieces included with
this unit
scissors
glue
oaktag
shoe box

Optional: clear plastic adhesive

To Prepare the Game:

1. The puzzle boards show scenes of sights you might see in Asia, Africa, Europe, and South America. Cut apart the four complete puzzle boards along the solid lines. Mount each one on a separate piece of oaktag. For durability, laminate or cover the puzzle boards with clear plastic adhesive.

2. Next cut apart the four sets of puzzle pieces along their outer edges only. Glue them onto oaktag and laminate them or cover them with clear plastic adhesive. Then cut the pieces apart.

3. When not in use, the puzzle boards and pieces can be stored in a shoe box.

How to Play:

For younger children:

1. Two to four children may play this game. Each child selects one puzzle board and places it in front of him or her.

2. Mix the puzzle pieces together and place them facedown in a pile in the center of the players.

3. Let the youngest child begin. He or she turns over the top puzzle piece and checks to see if it matches part of the scene on his or her puzzle board. If the piece does not belong to the scene on the puzzle board, the player turns it facedown and puts it on the bottom of the pile.

4. Play continues clockwise, each player drawing a puzzle piece and trying to match it to his or her puzzle board. The first player to piece together the entire scene on his or her puzzle board is the winner.

For older children:

1. Two to four children may play this game. Have the players mix the puzzle pieces together and lay them facedown in four rows of six pieces.

2. Each of the players chooses a puzzle board and places it in front of him or her.

3. The youngest child takes the first turn. He or she turns over one puzzle piece. If it matches a part of the player's puzzle board, he or she places it on top of that area of the board. If the piece does not match, the player turns it facedown again in its original place. Players must try to remember what is shown on each piece turned facedown again.

4. The game continues clockwise, with players taking turns flipping over pieces to see if they match their puzzle boards. The first player to piece together all the parts of the scene on his or her puzzle board becomes the winner.

Variation:

In their free time, individual children may put together the puzzle pieces to make the different scenes.